SPORTS' TOP MVPS™

SIDNEY CROSBY

WITHDRAWN

DON RAUF

rosen publishing's
rosen central®

New York

Published in 2019 by The Rosen Publishing Group, Inc.
29 East 21st Street, New York, NY 10010

Library of Congress Cataloging-in-Publication Data

Names: Rauf, Don, author.
Title: Sidney Crosby / Don Rauf.
Description: New York : Rosen Central, 2019. | Series: Sports' Top MVPs | Includes bibliographical references and index. | Audience: Grades: 5–8.
Identifiers: LCCN 2017050384| ISBN 9781508182016 (library bound) | ISBN 9781508182023 (paperback)
Subjects: LCSH: Crosby, Sidney, 1987– —Juvenile literature. | Hockey players—Canada—Biography—Juvenile literature.
Classification: LCC GV848.5.C76 R38 2019 | DDC 796.962092 [B] —dc23
LC record available at https://lccn.loc.gov/2017050384

Manufactured in the United States of America

On the cover: Sidney Crosby warms up before Game Five of the Eastern Conference First Round during the 2017 NHL Stanley Cup Playoffs.

CONTENTS

In the world of hockey, Sidney Crosby ranks as one of the best players. He is one of the most award winning of all time. Even from the time he was a toddler, "Sid the Kid" was a prodigy on ice. At age thirty, after having won the Stanley Cup three times, his star is still shining bright. Speed, skill, smarts, strength—Crosby has it all. He was born with a natural ability to skate, handle a stick, and fire a puck into a net. Crosby became the youngest National Hockey League (NHL) captain at that time at age nineteen and the youngest to lead his team to a Stanley Cup title. Crosby holds the record as the youngest player to reach two hundred career points and one hundred points in a single season. The superstar joined the exclusive Triple Gold Club when he captured an Olympic gold medal and won gold in the International Ice Hockey Federation World Championship (IIHF). "He's now in that group of top three, four all-time greats," Penguins general manager Jim Rutherford said in an interview on NHL.com.

In 2010, the twenty-three-year-old Crosby was burning up the ice in a twenty-five-game point streak. He tallied an incredible fifty-point run. In his rookie season playing against the Phoenix Coyotes, Crosby fell and still scored. One of his most incredible goals came in 2017, with a one-handed back-handed score against the Buffalo Sabres. Although his job is to play center and score goals, Crosby does whatever it takes to win. In the 2010 playoffs against the Ottawa Senators, Crosby dove to block a puck, making a critical save—his team would go on to victory in the six-game series.

Like any athlete, Crosby has had to battle through discouraging slumps as well. For several years before 2016,

Sidney Crosby was one of the youngest captains in the National Hockey League. On his jersey with the Pittsburgh Penguins, he wears the number 87 for his birthday, which is 8/7/1987.

Crosby and the Penguins seemed to be fading. They just weren't winning like they used to. But grit, determination, and endless practice turned things around and brought them back to the Stanley Cup finals two years in a row. The young athlete also has had to deal with crippling concussions. These head injuries caused him to miss forty-eight games in the 2010–2011 season and twenty games at the start of the 2011–2012 season. Through it all, Crosby has stayed humble, modest, and true to his hometown roots, always returning to Cole Harbour, Nova Scotia, where he grew up and learned to master the sport.

"The biggest thing for me is the passion that I've always had for hockey," said Crosby. "I remember growing up, no matter what I did in life, my parents always told me to try to do my best at it and be my best. I can say going through different things that that passion is the most important part. It's not skills or talent or any of that stuff."

CHAPTER ONE

A NATURAL-BORN SKATER

If you go to the Nova Scotia Sport Hall of Fame in Canada, you'll see a curious sight: a clothes dryer riddled with black marks and dents. That dryer has become a symbol of the hard work it takes to succeed in professional sports. It once sat in Sidney Crosby's family home.

When the hockey hero was growing up, his parents, Troy and Trina, set up a makeshift hockey rink in their unfinished basement. It was complete with lines painted on the floor and a hockey net. Sidney spent endless hours there honing his slap shot. His friends would come over, too—often on rainy days. They would put on roller blades and practice, practice, practice.

When Sidney missed a shot, however, the Whirlpool would take the blow. A loud clang would resound throughout the house. Crosby said that his parents didn't get upset as long as the dryer kept working.

As a top player in the National Hockey League at age eighteen, Crosby was invited to appear on *The Tonight Show*. For a gag, the host, Jay Leno, asked Crosby to shoot pucks into a dryer. Ironically, many thought the appliance had served as his goal growing up, but it really was the object that took the brunt of all his missed shots.

His parents also didn't mind the dryer getting banged up because they were devoted hockey fans. His mother has two brothers who

The dryer from Sidney Crosby's childhood home bears the marks from his missed practice shots.

were avid players—one tried out for a minor league team in the Canadian Hockey League (CHL).

Sidney's father competed in the Quebec Major Junior Hockey League, and in 1984, the Montreal Canadiens drafted him as a goalie. Other work opportunities, however, took Troy in another direction, and he never had the chance to play in an NHL game.

BABY BOTTLE IN ONE HAND, STICK IN THE OTHER

Sidney Patrick Crosby coasted into the world on August 7, 1987, also written 8/7/87. (That's why his jersey number is 87.) Although he wasn't born wearing a pair of skates, he seemed to have hockey in his blood from day one. In fact, a photo at the Nova Scotia Sport Hall of Fame shows the baby Sidney drinking from a bottle while holding a hockey stick.

When he laced up his first pair of skates at age three, the future star athlete appeared to be a natural. He almost instantly mastered the basics of stick handling. "One of the first times he was on the ice, the other kids were wobbling around but he was shooting the puck off the boards," his father said.

His father encouraged him and gave him his full support in pursuing the sport. Although Sidney originally wanted to be a goalie like his father, his dad steered him to be a forward. A forward's main role is to assist and score goals.

Troy taught Sidney all he knew, and the young hockey fan absorbed everything about the game like a sponge. Downtime was often spent together in front of the TV watching the Montreal Canadiens compete. When a game wasn't on, his dad might pop in a video like "Gretzky's Greatest Goals" about Canada's legendary hockey star.

SID THE KID

As a toddler, Sidney demonstrated his special gift for the game playing on a Timbits Hockey team. The Tim Hortons donut chain started this program for children ages four to eight. Tim Horton himself was a stellar athlete like Crosby and grew up dreaming to be an NHL hockey player.

The Early Years
In the basement of his Cole Harbour home, a three year old Sid the Kid.

Even as a three-year-old, Sidney excelled at ice skating and showed impressive stick-handling skills for a child his age.

By age six, Sidney was competing with the Novice-level Cole Harbour AAA Red Wings, and he won his first trophy. In an interview with the CBC, a coach for the Wings said that he received a call from Sidney's father one day. Troy asked the coach if his five-year-old could be moved up to play with the six-year-olds. The coach was skeptical at first, but when he came to check out the young Sidney, he was blown away. He saw a youngster with such control, poise, and skill that he could easily play with older skaters.

Sidney began setting records at age seven. Over the course of fifty-two games, he scored thirty-four goals and made fourteen assists. (An assist is shooting, passing, or deflecting the puck toward a teammate who scores.) In an interview with the Halifax *Daily News*, the youngster said, "They say you have to do your best and work hard and things will happen. You can make it if you try."

YOUTH HOCKEY LEAGUES IN CANADA

The levels of youth hockey in Canada are divided according to the following categories. Within these age categories are teams with different skill levels, with AAA being the highest caliber.

Initiation (Timbits)—ages five and six
Novice—ages seven and eight
Atom—ages nine and ten
Peewee—ages eleven and twelve
Bantam—ages thirteen and fourteen
Midget—ages fifteen to seventeen
Junior/Juvenile—ages eighteen and nineteen

Sidney worked hard off the ice as well—keeping up an A average and being friendly to all his fellow students. He took time to be extra kind to special-needs kids at his school, too.

When he reached the Atom level league for ages nine and ten, Sidney led the Red Wings to two provincial championships two seasons in a row. The ten-year-old scored 159 goals in a fifty-five-game schedule—an incredible record.

The following year, at the Peewee level, he made it to the Quebec International Peewee Tournament. By then, his reputation as a "must-see" player was spreading. He made the All-Star Team and led his Red Wings beyond the provincial championship to become the Atlantic champions.

CHAPTER TWO

A TEEN TITAN

At fourteen, Sidney was wowing crowds and coaches making miraculous plays with his midget AAA hockey team called the Subways. Although most of his teammates were three years older, Sidney captured the tournament MVP at the Air Canada Cup National Championship—the youngest player ever to take that title.

In an interview that year on the Canadian talk show *The Hour*, Sid the Kid said, "My game is making plays, making things happen, and scoring goals. Getting paid to do something you love to do [like play professional hockey]—I can't even imagine how amazing that would be."

To further develop his skills, Sidney left his beloved Canada to attend Shattuck-St. Mary's, a prep school in Minnesota known for its excellent hockey program. The school had been the training ground for an impressive roster of future NHL players. For the 2002–2003 season, the sophomore Sidney again outshined the others with seventy-two goals in fifty-seven games.

Although his time at St. Mary's was brief, the fifteen-year-old Sidney met fellow sophomore Jack Johnson at the school. The two hockey players became fast friends, and Johnson now plays for the Columbus Blue Jackets as a defenseman. "There literally was nothing we'd do together that wouldn't turn into a competition," Johnson said in an article in the Minneapolis *Star Tribune*.

In 2003, the gifted one was moving fast. The sixteen-year-old decided to grab the opportunity to play major junior league hockey. He

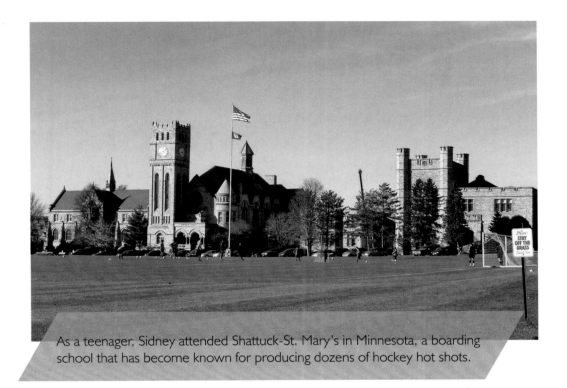

As a teenager, Sidney attended Shattuck-St. Mary's in Minnesota, a boarding school that has become known for producing dozens of hockey hot shots.

said goodbye to St. Mary's and moved back to Canada, where he continued to take required high school classes and ended up graduating from Harrison Trimble High School in New Brunswick in 2005.

He started with the Quebec Major Junior Hockey League, drafted by the Rimouski Oceanic team to play center. Rookies don't always get a lot of ice time, but the Oceanic knew they had an extraordinary player and frequently put him in the game. He led the league in scoring two years in a row, taking first place in goals, assists, and points.

At sixteen, Sidney sailed into the Hockey World Junior Championships, held in the winter of 2003–2004. The annual event organized by the IIHF features the world's best male players under twenty years of age playing in teams that represent their countries. His first year in the competition, the Canadian team fell to its US competitors. They were feeling confident and were ahead of the US

TEAM POSITIONS

In a hockey game, six players are on each team, and they play one of three positions.

Forwards. The three forwards try to get through the opposing team's defense to make the goals or assist in getting the goals. There is a center forward (like Sidney), a right wing, and a left wing. The centers are often the fastest and strongest on the team. They must be good at shooting, passing, and working both ends of the ice.

Defenders. The two defenders try to block opposing team members from scoring and they usually help guard the net with one on the left side and one on the right side.

Goalies. The goalie on each team stays in front of the net. His job is to keep the other team from scoring. Goaltenders may be the bravest team members—they must block vulcanized rubber pucks that can come at them at more than 100 miles per hour (160 kilometers per hour). Goaltenders wear masks and specialized protective gear designed to absorb the blow from a forcefully fired puck and prevent injury.

team at first, but as Sidney said, "All of a sudden, things turn quickly and you're disappointed."

CHAMPIONSHIPS

The following year's world championships for Crosby were far different. During the competition, Sid the Kid dazzled the crowd with six goals and three assists, leading his team to tournament gold. He called the win one of his most memorable hockey moments.

After defeating Sweden and other teams, Sidney took his country to a gold-medal win with a final battle against Russia during the Ice Hockey World Junior Championships.

In 2004, Sidney was tempted to take a multimillion-dollar contract with the World Hockey Association, a major professional league that was proposed to rival the NHL. He decided he wasn't quite mature enough to take that on. So he returned to the Rimouski Oceanic.

Sid's superstar skills next helped take his team to the major junior ice hockey championship in May 2005. Although taking home the prestigious Memorial Cup would have put a feather in his helmet, even the best teams and players cannot win all the time. The Oceanic faced off against the London Knights in the deciding game and suffered a crushing 4–0 loss. Sidney took the defeat hard.

"I'm tired and disappointed. It's been a long season," Sidney said in an interview on the London Knights website.

Still, even in losing, Sidney knew the value of good sportsmanship and gave the other team praise: "They did a good job checking us. They knew what we could do with our speed and they just slowed us right down. You have to give them credit. They did a good job."

Still, for hockey fans looking for the next big thing, Sidney was it. Wayne Gretzky, who was nicknamed "the Great One," soon dubbed Sidney "the Next One."

Sid could have gone on to college with scholarships from many top schools. (Because he always valued academics, he later took a history course at Southern New Hampshire University and wrote a final paper on World War II.) But in 2005, at age eighteen, Crosby was on course to be drafted by the National Hockey League, an opportunity he couldn't turn down.

As high school was coming to an end, Sidney was ready to join the big league. Just shy of his eighteenth birthday, Sidney went on to be selected first overall in the draft by the Pittsburgh Penguins on July 30, 2005. Because every team in the National Hockey League had been eager to get the wunderkind Sidney, the 2005 draft was nicknamed "The Sidney Crosby Sweepstakes."

CHAPTER THREE

FROM RISING ROOKIE TO SUPERSTAR

C rosby skated into Pittsburgh when the team and the fans sorely needed a lift. They had good reason for feeling disheartened. Recent times had been bleak for the Penguins. For three straight years, they were at the bottom of the league. Ticket sales were low. The Mellon Arena was desperately in need of repairs. Struggling financially, the franchise was forced to auction off its best players. One of the only bright spots for Pittsburgh was Mario Lemieux. The legendary Hall of Fame center was so dedicated to the Penguins that he had bought the team and was doing everything in his power to reenergize the flagging enterprise.

In the 2003–2004 season, the Penguins ranked dead last—officially the worst team in the National Hockey League. Then the 2004–2005 season was completely canceled because of a labor dispute. It was the first time the Stanley Cup was not awarded since 1919. What was bad news for all of hockey may have oddly been good luck for the Penguins. The Penguins needed a savior, and the time was just right for them to get one. When the draft for the 2005 season came along, the Penguins were perfectly poised to snatch up Sidney.

His signing was the ray of hope that not only lifted team spirits, but gave the city of Pittsburgh a new optimism. In fact, after a yearlong

As a seventeen-year-old Canadian hockey phenom, Crosby gave the last-ranked Pittsburgh Penguins a desperately needed lift when they nabbed him in the 2005 NHL Entry Draft.

hockey drought, fans all over were hoping that Sidney could pump new life back into the sport. That would be a lot to shoulder for most seventeen-year-olds, but Sidney took it in stride. He was doing what he loved—he was focused on playing the game and giving his best.

At 5 feet 11 inches (1.8 meters) and 200 pounds (90.7 kilograms), he was hardly the biggest guy on the ice. His trainer said in an interview in *Hockey News* that he wasn't the strongest or fastest, but he could combine multiple movements in training and translate them into game situations. Plus, he had the confidence and skills to match or even surpass those more experienced than he was.

When he arrived for training in August, reporters and photographers surrounded him. He had already appeared on *The Tonight Show* with Jay Leno and signed multimillion-dollar deals with Reebok and Gatorade. His face was plastered on posters and magazines, including an article in *GQ*.

A MENTOR SHOWS THE WAY

Crosby said that he was a bit awestruck his first couple days of training with the Penguins. He had grown up idolizing Mario Lemieux, whose poster had hung on his bedroom wall in Canada. Lemieux took the fledgling Penguin under his wing. Crosby's first season would be Lemieux's last as a player. Now forty, Lemieux had suffered from a heart condition and battled Hodgkin's disease. But before he hung up his jersey for good, he wanted to make sure the Crosby would transition into the NHL with ease. The two not only gained a relationship as teammates on the ice, but also outside the arena as well. During the first few years of his playing seasons, Crosby lived with Lemieux and his family in their home in Pittsburgh. "When you get to know him, he is such a down-to-earth guy," Crosby said in an interview.

OFF TO A STRONG START

In his debut season, it took a while for Crosby to find his stride. The team lost their first nine games. Crosby also got pegged as a whiner by some critics. In the beginning, he complained about a lot of the calls made by the referees. Fans chalked it up to youthful inexperience. Soon, though, Crosby was talking less and scoring more. By December, he led

HOCKEY SHOTS

There are four basic shots in NHL hockey.

Slap shot. A slap shot is a hard shot made by raising the stick about waist high before striking the puck with a sharp slapping motion. It can reach speeds of over 100 miles per hour (160 km/h) and has more power but is usually less accurate than a wrist shot. It's also the hardest shot for a player to get right. The hardest recorded ice hockey shot in any competition was a 110.3 mile-per-hour (177.5 km/h) slap shot by Denis Kulyash of Russia. Goalies dread the slap shot.

Wrist shot. A wrist shot is a controlled, accurate shot using the arm and wrist to fire a puck forward from the concave side of the hockey stick blade.

Backhand shot. Taken from the backside of the blade, the backhand is less accurate and less powerful than a forehand but can be effective in confusing goalies.

Snap shot. Abbreviated type of wrist shot requiring a quick snap of the wrists while the puck rests in place.

the team in scoring and was named assistant captain, a prestigious title for an eighteen-year-old.

He started racking up the goals and assists at a frenetic pace, ending his rookie season with 102 points. That season, he was one of the leading scorers, finishing sixth, and was the youngest NHL player to reach the 100-point mark.

Crosby also brought a jolt of excitement back to Pittsburgh. The team played to sell-out crowds in twelve games in an arena that could handle just over 17,000 fans. Overall, an average of 15,804 fans attended each game.

STILL A LOSING SEASON

At the end of the season, however, Crosby's star power was not enough to lift the team out of the basement. They finished in last place in the Atlantic Division and did not make the playoffs.

Crosby recognized and accepted losing as part of the game, but he vowed to keep pushing and making the team better. In an interview with the Pittsburgh *Post-Gazette*, he said, "Teams will go through some times that are hard. You can't give up. You have to make sure you keep trying to improve." And that's exactly what the Penguins did.

THE TURNAROUND

"Anytime you start a new one [season], you have to erase the year before," Crosby said at the beginning of his second year. "I think that's what I am going to do and I think that's what we all should do."

It had been five years since they made it that far, but the Penguins aggressively pushed ahead in 2006–2007 to finally make the playoffs. Although they fell to the Ottawa Senators in five games, Crosby notched an impressive 120 points for the year, achieving 200 career points before the end of the season, making him the youngest NHL player to reach that milestone.

In May 2007, after the playoffs ended, the nineteen-year-old was named captain, the youngest in NHL history at the time. "I understand there's going to be a lot more responsibility on my shoulders with this but I think its something I'm ready for. I was always told that age is just a number and I've never tried to let it get in the way of anything. I try to lead by example." Although Pittsburgh was humbled by the playoff loss, things were looking up with Captain Sid at the helm.

The following year, the hockey renaissance in Pittsburgh was in full swing with the Mellon Arena selling out all forty-one home games for the first time in Penguin history. That season, Crosby became the youngest winner of the Art Ross Trophy, with his league-leading 120 points (thirty-six goals, eighty-four assists). Captain Sid led his scrappy team all the way to the Stanley Cup finals, the Penguins' first appearance in sixteen years. Although Crosby missed twenty-nine games due to injuries during the season, he competed in the playoffs for the final Stanley Cup battle. Despite an impressive drive, the Detroit Redwings defeated the Penguins in six games. Crosby still left as a shining star, tying for top scorer in the playoffs.

REACHING THE TOP

Even with a playoff loss, the trajectory for the Penguins was upward heading into the 2008–2009 season. Again, Crosby led his team to the finals. As fate would have it,

At age nineteen, Crosby became the youngest NHL captain at the time and led the once last-place Penguins all the way to the Stanley Cup finals in the 2007–2008 season.

they again faced the Detroit Redwings. Duking it out in the best of seven series, things didn't look promising for the Penguins when the Redwings took a 3–2 advantage. But Pittsburgh fought back to tie, forcing a final climactic showdown on enemy turf in Detroit.

In the last game, the twenty-one-year-old Crosby took a hard hit against the boards and spent very little time on the ice. Even without him, Pittsburgh conquered Detroit, and Crosby celebrated his first NHL championship win. He credited his teammates for the Stanley Cup victory, singling out Pittsburgh goalie Marc-Andre Fleury for making a stellar twenty-three saves. And despite sitting out most of Game 7, Crosby recorded the most goals scored in the playoffs.

"It's unbelievable. It's the stuff you dream of as a kid. It's reality now," said the youngest captain to win the Stanley Cup. "We worked so hard. It's amazing to see how far we've come, and I couldn't feel any better."

GOING FOR THE GOLD

How could Crosby go any higher? The answer came with the 2010 Winter Olympics in Vancouver. The gold medal battle came down to one game—the

Canada took Olympic gold with a 3–2 win over the United States when Crosby made an overtime goal in one of the most-watched games in hockey history.

United States vs. Canada. For sports fans, this was the event of the season. It was rated as the most-watched television broadcast in Canadian history, with nearly half of the Canadian population watching the entire game and about 80 percent of Canadians viewing at least part of the game. It was also the most-watched hockey game in the United States in thirty years.

In the second period, as the United States fell behind, 2–0, Canada was feeling confident that victory was near. The United States wouldn't wilt, however. The United States thundered back to tie things up with just twenty-four seconds on the clock. As the game went into overtime, the nail-biter of a game put fans on the edge of their seats. Seven minutes and forty seconds in, Crosby screamed to Jarome Iginia to pass the puck. Iginia sent it over and Crosby fired. The puck sailed through the US goalie's legs. Score! The largely Canadian crowd erupted. Hockey fans dubbed the shot "the golden goal." All within a year, Crosby, now just twenty-two years of age, had won a Stanley Cup and an Olympic gold medal.

CHAPTER FOUR

OVERCOMING OBSTACLES

Crosby was skating into the 2010–2011 season at an all-time high. As someone who had played the sport his whole life, Crosby always knew that the speed and power required made it a dangerous sport. There's lots of body contact as players slam into each other racing on skates around the rink. Plus, fights often break out and players can get pummeled.

The aggressive aspect of the game can cause back pain, plus pulled hamstrings, groin pulls, strained calves, and all manner of sprains, bruises, and scrapes plague players. Serious spinal injuries are a threat as well. In 2016, Matt Olson, a twenty-year-old player for the Chicago Cougars of the US Premier Hockey League (USPHL) flew at full speed headfirst into the boards. The injury left him paralyzed below the shoulders. Another potentially grave injury in hockey comes from concussions.

HAMPERED BY A HEAD INJURY

Crosby had suffered his fair share of bang-ups but nothing was ever too serious. On the first day of 2011, that changed. Crosby and his team were competing against rival Alex Ovechkin and his Washington Capitals

A MAN OF MANY NICKNAMES

Like many sports heroes, Crosby has been tagged with a few nicknames along his road to success.

The Next One. Even early on, hockey fans thought Sidney was
showing talent equal to hockey superstar Wayne Gretzky, who was
known as the Great One. Gretzky and others started calling him the
Next One.

Sid the Kid. He earned this title for his youthfulness.

Darryl. "Not too many guys know about it now, but when I was
in junior, my first exhibition game I got eight points, and [Hall of
Famer] Darryl Sittler got 10 in the NHL [in a game in 1976], so
they just said 'Darryl' and it kind of stuck the last couple of years,"
Crosby told the Pittsburgh *Post-Gazette*. "That's how nicknames
come, in funny ways like that."

---

in a game called the Winter Classic. The Capitals' David Steckel blindsided
Crosby, hammering him hard to the head in a collision. Crosby dropped
to the ice and wobbled back to the bench. Crosby basically shrugged off
the hit and continued to play in the days to come. On January 5, in a game
against Tampa Bay, Victor Hedman drove Crosby hard into the boards.
The following day, the Penguins coach announced that Crosby had a mild
concussion. It's not uncommon for symptoms to develop or worsen a day
or more after the initial hit that causes brain trauma.

The head injury was serious. Crosby suffered headaches, spatial
and balance problems, and mental fogginess. Crosby described this as a
"roller-coaster" experience. The concussion forced him to miss the rest

WELCOME BACK SID

Crosby has missed more than one hundred games in his career due to concussion-related issues. After 320 days of recovery in 2011, fans welcomed him back to the ice.

of the season, and many speculated as to whether or not he would ever return to the game. His concussion put the issue of hockey head injuries in the spotlight. Sports fans and players debated the violence of the game and how to improve player safety.

Fortunately, as the start of a new season approached in the fall of 2011, Crosby showed improvement. He took part in the Penguins' annual tradition of personally delivering season tickets to the homes of fans and hit the ice for a few practices. Still, he was unsure about continuing to play.

Then on November 21, 2011, the big day for hockey fans arrived. After 320 days of recovery, Crosby finally returned to play against the New York Islanders. Within six minutes on the ice, he delivered his first goal. Although "the Kid" was back, he was still not at full strength. Two weeks later, he was sidelined again when concussionlike symptoms returned. He played only twenty-two games in 2011 and 2012. Still, Pittsburgh had faith in their boy and signed him to a contract that summer that made him the highest-paid player in the NHL.

A HIT IN THE FACE

Crosby returned stronger for the 2012–2013 season, but again calamity struck. During this shortened NHL season caused by a labor dispute, Crosby took another serious physical blow at the end of March in a game against the Islanders. A slap shot by one of his own teammates deflected off a stick, sending the puck into Crosby's face.

Crosby dropped, with teeth and blood spilling onto the ice. The force of the puck broke his jaw and damaged ten teeth. Hockey's famous face required intense medical and dental work. After about two months of recuperating and dropping about 10 pounds (4.5 kg) from a largely liquid diet, Crosby returned in time for the playoffs. The next year, Crosby rebounded for a strong season in 2013–2014, leading the NHL in points with 104. The following year, he put in a strong performance but tallied only 84 points. The team barely made the playoffs, and then the New York Rangers came back from a three-games-to-one deficit to obliterate the Penguins in the first round of the Stanley Cup playoffs.

Raising the trophy for the International Ice Hockey World Championship, Crosby and his teammates celebrated Canada's win over Russia on May 17, 2015.

While 2015 may have been lackluster for the Penguins, Crosby joined the very exclusive Triple Gold Club in May. As captain, he took Team Canada to first place in the International Ice Hockey Federation World Championship.

Still, seven years had passed since Crosby had taken his team to the Stanley Cup finals, and he hoped to get his team on course to start winning again.

CHAPTER FIVE

SKATING BACK TO VICTORY

In the first few months of the 2015–2016 season, Crosby was worried. He only made a handful of points and wasn't among the NHL's scoring leaders. Sportswriters were calling it the worst scoring slump of his career. *Sports Illustrated* wrote that midway through the season, the Penguins were "touch-and-go" to make the playoffs. Crosby said he had to answer some hard questions about his playing and the team as a whole.

"Nothing we did seemed to work," Crosby wrote in an article in the Cauldron. "Offensively we struggled and with each frustrating loss, we fell further and further behind the competition."

On top of it all, reporters kept showing up to ask him why the team wasn't scoring. Crosby said that, slowly, he began to adjust his game and the hundreds of hours of practice with the team began to pay off.

A CHANGE FOR THE BETTER

In December, a new coach, Mike Sullivan, came in and the switch-up reenergized the team. Gradually, the wins started coming. "Sullivan gave me opportunities to try to work my way back into things," said Sidney on NHL.com. "He was just good at holding everyone accountable, myself included, and making sure that I got better."

After struggling through a career slump, Crosby came roaring back to form in the 2015–2016 season, taking the Pittsburgh Penguins to another Stanley Cup win.

The fan site Pensburgh wrote that Crosby kicked it into high gear in January, looking "reinvigorated, focused and dangerous just about every shift." Each month in the new year, he performed better than the last. He ended the regular season leading the club in scoring, with a solid showing of thirty-six goals and forty-nine assists.

In the beginning of April, Pittsburgh shut out the New York Islanders with a 5–0 win to clinch a playoff spot. After having lost to the Rangers in the past two playoffs, the Penguins finally got their revenge, eliminating New York in five games. They went on to knock off the Tampa Bay Lightning, with Crosby delivering three game-winning goals.

The team that had started the season floundering on the bottom had charged its way back to the top to face the San Jose Sharks for the Stanley Cup. The Penguins won the series in six games, with the final goal coming as Crosby passed the puck to teammate Kris Letang, who rifled it in for the game-winning point. Crosby added another MVP award to his growing mountain of honors.

ANOTHER SEASON OF BRUISES AND WINS

With a Stanley Cup in hand, the Penguins began the 2016–2017 season feeling confident—a nice way to enter their fiftieth anniversary season. Crosby wrote in *Sports Illustrated*: "I won't rest on my laurels. I just can't. Winning is special. If last season taught me anything, it was how thin the line is between being 'washed up' and lifting the Stanley Cup. I don't want to struggle like that again."

Although battered from recent injuries, Crosby led his team to another Stanley Cup win in the 2016–2017 season.

But Crosby faced a major challenge before official play even began. During a practice in early October, he suffered another concussion. This time the blow wasn't as severe as before, so Crosby was back on the ice in a few weeks. He went on to have one of his best seasons, netting forty-four goals and reaching a personal best for shooting for a full season. In February 2017, he became one of the eighty-six players to have ever reached the 1,000-point mark.

In clinching a spot in the playoffs competing against the Buffalo Sabres, Crosby both made an amazing shot and paid a price. At the end of the first period, he made what some have called a nearly impossible one-handed backhanded goal, scooping the puck off the ice with his stick and throwing it into the net, a technique some call the Crosby move. Although his team savored victory that night, Crosby's celebration was muted. Crosby took a stick to the mouth—knocking out two front teeth. Still, the Penguins wrapped up a playoff berth for an impressive eleventh consecutive season.

LIGHTNING STRIKES TWICE

In May, during the Eastern Conference semifinals, Sid the Kid was diagnosed with another concussion when he took a cross-check from one of the Washington Capitals. Luckily, he missed only one game and was back to help the Penguins take the series.

Next up, the Penguins faced the Ottawa Senators in the Eastern Conference final, but the chance to go to the finals looked touch-and-go as the team battled it out in a final seventh game. The last game was truly exciting, going into double overtime until Crosby's teammate Chris Kunitz delivered the deciding goal.

In June, the Penguins went up against the Nashville Predators in the Stanley Cup finals. In the first four games, the teams were tied, with two wins each. But in Game 5, Crosby shifted the momentum, delivering some dazzling assists that gave the Penguins a 6–0 win. Keeping up the pressure in Game 6, Crosby and his teammates captured their second Stanley Cup win in a row. His strong postseason performance also earned him the Conn Smythe Trophy as most valuable playoff player for the second consecutive time. Crosby had eight goals and twenty-seven points in the twenty-four games of this playoff run.

Crosby has earned his place among the hockey greats. Here he is with the Conn Smythe Trophy for most valuable player and the Rocket Richard Trophy for leading goal scorer in 2017.

AGE IS JUST A NUMBER

When Crosby turned thirty on August 7, 2017, he had already become the most-decorated hockey athlete of his time, with three Stanley Cups, two Olympic gold medals, a World Cup of Hockey medal, and numerous other awards. He has even been featured on a Canadian stamp.

At this age in hockey, many players hang up their skates. In fact, the hockey statistic site QuantHockey.com says that the average retirement

TIME OFF THE ICE

When it's time to relax, Crosby likes to spend time with his family, friends, his girlfriend, model Kathy Leutner, and his yellow Labrador, Sam. He loves to eat fast food like pizza and says he "crushes" Tim Hortons Timbits (the bite-size donut morsels). He grew up fishing and still enjoys the pastime.

In 2015, he opened a hockey school in his Canadian hometown to train a new generation of hockey stars. Crosby also believes in giving as much time to charitable work as he can. He has worked with the Make-a-Wish Foundation, Big Brothers/Big Sisters, and the Special Olympics. He has taken time to make friends with youngsters who are battling cancer. "People from my hometown have always made it a point to give back," Crosby said in the Pittsburgh *Post-Gazette* in 2017. "I always told myself that, if I ever get to this point, I would do the same." Crosby visits kids in the local Children's Hospital and participates in (and helps fund) the Little Penguins Learn to Play program.

age for an NHL player is twenty-eight. But Crosby still believes what he said when he was a teen: age is just a number and shouldn't be a block to success. As young, talented players come in, Crosby is determined to match their skills. He works on his skating constantly to keep up with their rapid pace.

"With all the young talent throughout the league, it just makes you want to get better yourself," Crosby said on the sports site the Cauldron. "I love having to adjust and adapt my game year-to-year to find ways to be my best."

FACT SHEET

Birthdate
August 7, 1987

Height
5 feet 11 inches (1.8 meters)

Weight
200 pounds (90.7 kg)

Team
Pittsburgh Penguins, Captain

Position
Center

Hometown
Cole Harbour, Nova Scotia

Achievements
- World Junior Cup gold medal winner in 2005.
- Selected by the Penguins in the 2005 NHL draft, becoming the youngest NHL player at the time.
- Youngest player to achieve a 100-point season, at age eighteen.
- Has accumulated more than 1,000 points in regular-season play.
- Winner of two Olympic gold medals and a World Cup Hockey gold medal.
- Selected for NHL All-Stars six times. Four Eastern Conference championships (2008, 2009, 2016, 2017). Two Conn Smythe trophies (2016, 2017). Two Art Ross trophies (2007, 2014). Two Rocket Richard trophies (2010, 2017). Three Ted Lindsay awards (2007, 2013, 2014). Two Hart trophies (2007, 2014).
- Has suffered several concussions but continues to be a top performer.
- Active with many charities, including his Sidney Crosby Foundation to benefit children in need.

TIMELINE

1987: Sidney Crosby is born on August 7.

2005: Crosby wins World Junior Ice Hockey Championships in January.

2005: He becomes the first draft pick by the Pittsburgh Penguins on July 30.

2006: Crosby becomes the youngest player to reach one hundred points.

2007: He becomes the youngest player to reach two hundred points. Crosby is named team captain at age nineteen.

2009: Crosby wins his first Stanley Cup on June 12.

2010: He wins his first Olympic gold medal.

2011: Crosby returns to play after a long recovery from head trauma November 21.

2014: He captures second Olympic gold medal on February 23.

2016: Crosby and the Penguins win the Stanley Cup, Crosby's second. He wins the World Cup of Hockey with Team Canada.

2017: Crosby and the Penguins win the Stanley Cup, Crosby's third. He reaches one thousand career points on February 16.

GLOSSARY

assist To pass or deflect the puck toward the scoring teammate.

boards The walls around a hockey rink, its shape is rectangular with rounded corners.

concussion A traumatic brain injury that is caused by a blow to the head or body, a fall, or other type of injury.

cross-check The act of using the shaft of a hockey stick between the two hands to forcefully disrupt an opponent.

deflect To cause the puck to change direction.

draft A process used in certain sports to select team players.

exhibition game An unofficial game, usually as part of preseason training or as a fund-raising event.

fledgling An inexperienced person.

franchise A team in a professional sports league.

hamstring Any of five tendons at the back of the knee.

lackluster Lacking vitality.

offense The action of trying to score.

playoff A competition played after the regular season by the top competitors to determine the league champion.

prodigy A young person with extraordinary talent.

reinvigorated Given new energy.

rookie A new recruit or player.

sideline To cause a player to be unable to play in a game.

trajectory The path followed by a flying object.

transition A process or period of changing.

vulcanized Hardened rubber or rubberlike material that is treated with sulfur at a high temperature.

wunderkind A person who achieves great success at an early age.

FOR MORE INFORMATION

American Collegiate Hockey Association
7638 Solution Center
Chicago, IL 60677-7006
Website: http://www.achahockey.org
This group supports the growth of collegiate hockey by providing struc-
    ture, regulating operations, and promoting quality.

Canadian Hockey League
305 Milner Avenue, Suite 201
Scarborough, Ontario M1B 3V4
Canada
(416) 332-9711
Website: http://www.chl.ca
Facebook: @CanadianHockeyLeague
Twitter: @CHLHockey
Instagram: @chlhockey
The world's largest developmental hockey league, with fifty-two
    Canadian and eight American teams participating—it oversees junior-
    level hockey and offers opportunities and assistance for serious
    junior-level players ages sixteen to twenty.

Hockey Canada
151 Canada Olympic Road SW, Suite 201
Calgary, Alberta T3B 6B7
Canada
(403) 777-3636
Website: http://www.hockeycanada.ca/en-ca/home
Facebook, Twitter, and Instagram: @HockeyCanada
The national governing body for grassroots hockey in Canada offers
    hockey programs, competitions, and news.

Hockey Hall of Fame
30 Yonge Street
Toronto, Ontario MSE 1X8
Canada
(416) 360-7735
Website: http://www.hhof.com
Facebook: @Hockey-Hall-of-Fame
Twitter: @HockeyHallFame
Instagram: @thehockeyhalloffame
The Hockey Hall of Fame celebrates the history of hockey and players.

International Ice Hockey Federation (IIHF)
Brandschenkestrasse 50
Postfach 1817
8027 Zurich, Switzerland
+41.44.562 22 00
Website: http://www.iihf.com
Facebook: @iihfhockey
Twitter: @IIHFHockey
This worldwide governing body for ice hockey offers news on champion-
    ship events around the globe.

National Hockey League (NHL)
1185 Avenue of the Americas
New York, NY 10036
(855) 438-0681
Website: http://www.nhl.com
Facebook: @NHL
Twitter, Instagram, and YouTube: @nhl
The NHL is a professional ice hockey league with twenty-four teams in
    the United States and seven in Canada. Its website offers news, ros-
    ters, stats, and schedules.

USA Hockey Foundation
Walter L. Bush, Jr. Center
1775 Bob Johnson Drive
Colorado Springs, CO 80906-4090
(719) 538-1165
Website: http://www.usahockeyfoundation.com
Facebook: @USAHockey
Twitter: @usahockey
YouTube: @USAHOCKEYHQ
This foundation makes grants to numerous Hockey for Everyone pro-
    grams, which assist young people to pursue hockey as a sport. The
    organization promotes safety and player development. It is the chari-
    table arm of USA Hockey.

FOR FURTHER READING

Buckley, James. *Scholastic Year in Sports 2017*. New York, NY: Scholastic, 2017.

Frederick, Shane. *Six Degrees of Sidney Crosby: Connecting Hockey Stars*. North Mankato, MN: Capstone Press, 2015.

Gitlin, Martin. *The Stanley Cup: All about Pro Hockey's Biggest Event*. North Mankato, MN: Capstone Press, 2012.

Hollingsworth, Paul. *Sidney Crosby: The Story of a Champion*. Halifax, Nova Scotia: Nimbus Publishing, 2017.

Kortemeier, Todd. *Make Me the Best Hockey Player*. Minneapolis, MN: SportsZone/Abdo Publishing, 2017.

Miller, Saul. *Hockey Tough*. 2nd ed. Champaign, IL: Human Kinetics, 2016.

Podnieks, Andrew. *Sid vs. Ovi: Natural Born Rivals*. Toronto, Ontario: McClelland & Stewart, 2011.

Redban, Bill. *Sidney Crosby: The Inspirational Story of Hockey Superstar Sidney Crosby*. North Charleston, SC: CreateSpace, 2014.

Southerland, Benjamin. *Sidney Crosby: A Biography of One of Hockey's Greatest Players*. North Charleston, SC: CreateSpace, 2015.

Winters, Jaime. *Center Ice: The Stanley Cup*. New York, NY: Crabtree Publishing Company, 2014.

BIBLIOGRAPHY

Adelson, Eric. "A League of His Own." ESPN the Magazine, February 15, 2008. http://www.espn.com/espnmag/story?id=3247072.

AP. "Penguins Beat Red Wings for Stanley Cup." CBS News, June 13, 2009. https://www.cbsnews.com/news/penguins-beat-red-wings-for -stanley-cup.

Baker, Katie. "The Timetable: Sidney Crosby's Lost Year." Grantland, October 6, 2011. http://grantland.com/features/sidney-crosby -lost-year.

Clarke, Mary. "Sidney Crosby's 30 Biggest Moments from His Road to NHL Stardom." SBNation, August 7, 2017. https://www.sbnation. com/nhl/2017/8/7/16095264/sidney"-crosby-happy-birthday-30 -best-moments-pittsburgh-penguins.

Cowan, Stu. "Sid (The Kid) Crosby Celebrates 26th Birthday." Montreal Gazette, August 7, 2013. http://montrealgazette.com/sports /sid-the-kid-crosby-celebrates-26th-birthday.

Crosby, Sidney. "Sidney Crosby: It's O.K. to Doubt Me; Sometimes I Even Doubt Myself." Sports Illustrated, the Cauldron, September 1, 2016. https://www.si.com/thecauldron/2016/09/01/sidney-crosby -pittsburgh-penguins-stanley-cup.

Goldberg, Rob. "Stanley Cup Final 2017: Top Highlights, Storylines from Penguins vs. Predators." Bleacher Report, June 12, 2017. http:// bleacherreport.com/articles/2715148-stanley-cup-final-2017-top -highlights-storylines-from-penguins-vs-predators.

Haberman, Darryl. "Saluting Crosby at 25: Facts and Figures." NHL.com, August 7, 2012. https://www.nhl.com/news/saluting -crosby-at-25-facts-and-figures/c-639346.

Kasan, Sam. "The Inside Scoop: Remembering the 2005 'Crosby' Draft." NHL.com, July 30, 2015 https://www.nhl.com/penguins/news /the-inside-scoop-remembering-the-2005-crosby-draft/c-776021.

Kasan, Sam. "Sidney Crosby: An Intimate Portrait (Sid the Man)." NHL

.com, July 27, 2017. https://www.nhl.com/penguins/news /sidney-crosby-an-intimate-portrait-sid-the-man/c-290516694.

Molinari, Dave. "Penguins Notebook: Crosby faced losing before." Pittsburgh Post-Gazette. December 9, 2005. http://www.post -gazette.com/sports/penguins/2005/12/09 /Penguins-Notebook-Crosby-faced-losing-before /stories/200512090149.

Orpik, Hooks. "When It Comes to Superstitions, Sidney Crosby Leads the Way Here Too." SBNation, Pensburgh, May 8, 2013. https:// www.pensburgh.com/2013/5/8/4313966/when-it-comes-to -superstitions-sidney-crosby-leads-the-way-here-too.

Rosen, Dan. "Sidney Crosby Solidifies Place among Greatest Ever with Third Cup Win." NHL.com, June 12, 2017. https://www.nhl.com /news/sidney-crosby-secures-place-among-greatest-ever-with -third-cup-win/c-289892518.

Shuker, Ronnie. "Why Sidney Crosby Is So Hard to Knock Off the Puck." The Hockey News, December 17, 2013. http://www.thehockeynews .com/news/article/why-sidney-crosby-is-so-hard-to-knock-off-the-puck.

Sidney Crosby Fan Site. "Sidney Crosby's Biography." Retrieved October 1, 2017. http://www.sidneycrosbyfans.info.

INDEX

ABOUT THE AUTHOR

Don Rauf is the author of numerous nonfiction books, including *Miguel Cabrera: Triple Crown Winner*, *Schwinn: The Best Present Ever*, *Killer Lipstick and Other Spy Gadgets*, *American Inventions*, *The French and Indian War*, *George Washington's Farewell Address*, and *Historical Serial Killers*. He lives in Seattle with his wife, Monique, and son, Leo.

PHOTO CREDITS